THE PONY CLUB
Quiz Book No. 3

A PONY CLUB PUBLICATION

© 2009 The Pony Club

Text by Toni Webber
Drawings by Maggie Raynor
Design by Jennie Smith

Produced for the Pony Club by
Barbara Cooper

A catalogue record of this book is available from
the British Library

Published by The Pony Club
Stoneleigh Park
Kenilworth
Warwickshire CV8 2RW

www.pcuk.org

Printed and bound in England
by Halstan & Company Limited

ISBN 978-0-9553374-6-8

Introduction

INTERBRANCH TEAM competitions are more popular than ever, but if a pony, however wonderful in every other way, is not a cross-country specialist, nor a show jumper, nor a games player, nor a dressage expert, a member's chances of being able to represent the branch are very limited. Fortunately, however, the interbranch quiz competition is now widespread, with at least two variations on a quiz theme leading to Pony Club championships.

Most team quizzes are aimed at mixed teams, with members drawn from at least three levels. A team may be made up of different age levels or different test standards, with each team member coming from a different group. Questions are then pitched at the appropriate level.

Compiling a quiz takes time and effort, and this, the third of the Pony Club quiz books, aims to make life a little easier for the "volunteer" assigned to produce one. Each of the quizzes it contains is divided into categories and each category has questions at different levels. The standards selected in every case are D, D+ level, C, C+ level and B Test and above. Categories may be selected from any of the quizzes, and the final contest can be as short or as long as you wish.

Some categories have questions with multiple-choice answers; in most a single answer is required.

Quiz No. 1

QUESTIONS ON:

*Horse and Pony Care; The Numbers Game
The Countryside; Around the World
Ancient Times; Health and Safety
Lucky Dip*

Horse and Pony Care

D, D+ STANDARD

1 How often should you check a field-kept pony?

2 What should you do to dried sugar beet pulp before feeding it to horses?

3 What is a metal curry comb used for?

4 Does a 12.2hh pony in light work (ie, out at grass and ridden for about an hour each day) need concentrates as well as grass or hay?

5 How often should you groom a pony that lives out?

C, C+ STANDARD

6 What is the combined system for keeping a pony?

7 How much time should be left between feeding a horse and working him?

8 What is the purpose of the body brush?

9 What percentage of concentrates should be given to a horse or pony in medium work (1½ hours' hacking daily, with active work including a Pony Club rally or competition)?

10 Why would you use a cactus cloth?

B & ABOVE

11 Cider vinegar can be used as a supplement to supply an important electrolyte. Which one?

12 Why should hay and straw be stacked on wooden, slatted pallets?

13 How much food per day would a 16.2hh horse weighing 600kgs require?

14 Which straw could form part of a horse's bulk food diet?

15 What would you use a wisp for?

The Numbers Game

D, D+ STANDARD

16 Over what distance is the Derby run?

17 How many players in a polocrosse team?

18 How many men did the Grand Old Duke of York lead to the top of the hill?

19 How many inches in a hand?

20 At what age (of the horse) does it become more difficult to be accurate when assessing his age?

The Countryside

C, C+ STANDARD

21 In what year was the Derby first run?

22 What is a horse's normal temperature?

23 How many horsemen of the Light Brigade rode into the "valley of death" at the Battle of Balaclava?

24 How many chukkas in a Gannon polo match?

25 What distance should be left for a pony between the two elements of a bounce fence?

B & ABOVE

26 The oldest classic race is the St. Leger. When was it first run?

27 At rest, a horse's heartbeat is normally between 35 and 45 beats per minute. To what number could it increase during fast or strenuous work?

28 In the 1890s, approximately how many horses worked in London (to the nearest 100)?

29 What is the ideal angle of the shoulder?

30 What size of stable is needed for a 16.2hh horse?

D, D+ STANDARD

31 What is the name given to the strip of land left fallow around the edge of a field?

32 If you are hacking out and pass through an open gate, should you shut it behind you?

33 What is the usual time of the year to see bluebells at their best?

34 What is the countryside code?

35 What should you do with ragwort?

C, C+ STANDARD

36 Why should you be particularly alert when riding in a heavily wooded area?

37 What is the difference between an Equinox (spring and autumn) and a Solstice (summer and winter)?

38 What is the main difference between a cart and a wagon?

39 Name three types of grass considered good for horses.

40 What is the ideal acreage for a pony?

B & ABOVE

41 When fording a stream, your horse starts pawing the water. What is he about to do?

42 What is a drove road?

43 Name three species of deer that live wild in the UK.

44 There is an old country saying, "When gorse is out of bloom, kissing is out of fashion." During which months would this apply?

45 *Tabanus bromia* is a particularly tiresome pest. What is it better known as?

Around the World

D, D+ STANDARD

46 In what country would you find a mustang?

47 Where do gauchos work?

48 Which horses are native to the marshland area near Marseilles?

49 Which state of the USA, famous for horse breeding, is known as the Blue Grass state?

50 By what name are the mounted troops of south-eastern Russia known?

C, C+ STANDARD

51 What major horse show takes place at Hickstead every July?

52 In India, what does a syce do?

53 In which country was the tiny pony, the Falabella, developed during the 20th century?

54 Where is the Spanish Riding School?

55 What are the feral or wild horses of North America called?

B & ABOVE

56 Which country has more horses than humans?

57 What is the name of the American race instituted in 1894 and regarded as the equivalent of the British Grand National?

58 Where would you find a brumby?

59 What name is given to the Russian three-horse sleigh?

60 What nation of the world has roughly three times as many polo players as any other nation?

Ancient Times

D, D+ STANDARD

61 What is the name of the winged horse of Greek mythology?

62 In which book of the Bible is it written, "Hast thou given the horse strength? Hast thou clothed his neck with thunder?"

63 How big was Eohippus, the earliest known horse, who lived about three million years ago?

64 Who is the Roman goddess of hunting?

65 What was the name of Alexander the Great's favourite charger?

C, C+ STANDARD

66 What is an onager?

67 Which people of the first millennium BC made elaborate head-dresses for their horses out of coloured felt?

68 Who are believed to be the first people to make iron horseshoes for their horses?

69 Who established the donkey in Europe?

70 Who is the Greek goddess of hunting?

B & ABOVE

71 Who is the Norse god of the hunt?

72 Who wrote *The Art of Horsemanship*?

73 What type of horse was the foundation of the English Thoroughbred?

74 Can you give the date – to the nearest 500 years – of the earliest domestication of horses?

75 Who was the first one-toed "horse" of ancient times?

Health and Safety

D, D+ STANDARD

76 When oiling a pony's hooves should you:
    (a) sit on the ground
    (b) crouch down
    (c) sit on your grooming box?

77 When is it compulsory to wear a body protector?
    (a) when competing across country in a Pony Club event
    (b) all the time
    (c) whilst grooming your pony

78 What should a horse be inoculated against?
    (a) equine influenza
    (b) tetanus
    (c) both

79 Before giving a pony a carrot what should you do?

    (a) wash and peel it

    (b) cut it into round slices

    (c) cut it into finger-shaped pieces

80 To make a pony pick up his foot, what should you do?

    (a) run your hand down the back of the leg whilst leaning against the leg to force his weight on to the other foot

    (b) give the hoof a good kick

    (c) tie a cord round the pastern and pull

C, C+ STANDARD

81 When tying up a haynet, should you:

    (a) tie the haynet rope to a metal wall-ring with a quick-release knot

    (b) first attach a string loop to the wall-ring and tie the haynet rope to that, using a quick-release knot

    (c) not bother with a haynet but scatter hay on the floor?

82 For what reason is a hunting tie (or stock) worn?

    (a) to look smart

    (b) to give extra support to the neck

    (c) to tie round your waist if you need added visibility when riding home in the dark

83 If a horse has been galloping (across country, for example), he will be feeling thirsty. Should you:

    (a) offer him as much as he can drink straightaway

    (b) wait until his breathing rate returns to normal, then offer him half a bucket

    (c) do not give him a drink at all but use the water to wash him down?

84 What is the safety stirrup with a removable rubber ring forming one side known as?

    (a) a Peacock safety stirrup

    (b) a Phoenix stafety stirrup

    (c) a Pheasant safety stirrup

85 When leading a horse from the ground along a road, should you:

    (a) lead from the near side, walking along the right-hand side of the road, thus placing yourself between the horse and the traffic

    (b) walk along the left-hand side of the road, but lead from the off side so that you are between the horse and the traffic, or

    (c) walk ahead of the horse along the left-hand side of the road?

B & ABOVE

86 All-terrain vehicles and motor cycles may be used on a showground provided the rider is wearing the appropriate headgear and is how old?

    (a) 15 or above

(b) 16 or above
(c) 17 or above

87 In what year did a team from Great Britain first take part in an exchange visit to the United States of America?
(a) 1953
(b) 1965
(c) 1981

88 At a mounted games friendly competition, which of these MUST be in attendance?
(a) a paramedic
(b) a trained first-aider
(c) a qualified first-aider

89 In a cross-country competition – at all levels – which of these must a rider wear?
(a) a body protector *and* a medical armband
(b) a body protector *or* a medical armband
(c) neither of these

90 If a rider has a fall and is unconscious, should you:
(a) remove the hat and place the rider in the recovery position
(b) leave the rider exactly as he or she has fallen and await the arrival of a medical team or
(c) leave the hat on and place the rider in the recovery position?

Lucky Dip

91 Who founded the Hickstead All-England Show Jumping course?

92 Where is Tattenham Corner?

93 Who is the goddess Epona and what is she the goddess of?

94 In the USA, what are the Breeders' Cup Races?

95 What is the native horse of Brittany, France?

96 Where would you find the stuffed body of Napoleon's horse, Marengo?

97 In which book does the horse Ginger appear?

98 What is meant by the term "closed season"?

99 If foot soldiers are infantry, what is the name given to those on horseback?

100 What do horses use incisors for?

Quiz No. 2

QUESTIONS ON:

*The Pony Club; Horses in Fiction
At the Races; Working Dogs
American/English; Colours and Markings
Lucky Dip*

The Pony Club

D, D+ STANDARD

101 What is the new test introduced by Headquarters for very young members?

102 Who is entitled to join the Pony Club as a Centre member?

103 What colour felt is worn when you have passed your D+ test?

104 Name two of the new Mini Achievement Awards.

105 When was the Pony Club formed?

C, C+ STANDARD

106 What are Badge Buddies?

107 The Pony Club in the UK and Northern Ireland is divided into how many areas?

108 What is the maximum amount of prize money which can be given in a Pony Club competition?

109 Which Branch won the Prince Philip Cup when it was first presented?

110 Is the Pony Club a registered charity?

B & ABOVE

111 What newspaper-run children's club gave Mrs Marchant, the wife of one of the Pony Club's founders, the inspiration for starting the Pony Club?

112 Who signs Efficiency Certificates?

113 When did the Pony Club separate from the British Horse Society?

114 Which was the first overseas Branch of the Pony Club?

115 Where in America was the first Pony Club Branch formed?

Horses in Fiction

D, D+ STANDARD
Name the following:

116 The black and white horse which carried Velvet Brown to victory in the Grand National in the book, *National Velvet*, by Enid Bagnold.

117 The grey horse ridden by the Lone Ranger, the masked man who anonymously restored law and order in the Wild West.

118 The striking palomino known as the Wonder Horse, the hero of a children's television series.

119 The black horse with a white star and one white foot, the hero of a book written by Anna Sewell in the 19th century.

120 Tom's little pony in Hilaire Belloc's *New Cautionary Tales*.

C, C+ STANDARD

121 The fleabitten grey known as the Past Pluperfect Prestissimo Player of Polo.

122 Don Quixote's horse, formerly a hack, who was "all skin and bones".

123 The fat little grey pony, who was cheerful, plucky and good-tempered and a favourite with Squire Gordon's two girls.

124 The farm horse in George Orwell's satirical novel, *Animal Farm*.

125 The hero of an epic poem by John Masefield, a big dark bay with a beautiful head and "a jumping bone".

B & ABOVE

126 The red-haired pony, bought for Jackanapes, who ended his days pulling a bath-chair up and down Goose Green in the sunshine.

127 The donkey with whom R L Stevenson journeyed in France in his book *Travels with a Donkey* in the Cévennes.

128 The hero of John Steinbeck's tragic tale about the love of a boy for his horse.

129 The race of horses discovered by Gulliver in *Gulliver's Travels* by Jonathan Swift.

130 The horse who belongs to a boy named Howard, who was bred and raised on a ranch in Wyoming.

At the Races

D, D+ STANDARD

131 At what racecourse would you find Becher's Brook?

132 What is the shortest distance for a flat race in Britain?

133 How many Classic races are there?

134 What is the governing body of racing?

135 In the Queen's racing colours, what is unusual about the hat-cover?

C, C+ STANDARD

136 What is a claiming jockey?

137 At what racecourse would you find the Rowley Mile?

138 Where is the St. Leger run?

139 What is the Paris-Mutuel?

140 What is the maximum number of runners allowed in the Grand National?

B & ABOVE

141 Name the three American Classic races which form the American Triple Crown.

142 Where is the Prix de l'Arc de Triomphe run?

143 At what racecourse would you find Swinley Bottom?

144 How many winners must an apprentice jockey ride to reduce his weight allowance from 7lb to 5lb?

145 What is a "bumper"?

Working Dogs

D, D+ STANDARD

146 The Beagle is bred to hunt what kind of animal?

147 Originally a cattle-herder, this type of dog is best known today as the Queen's favourite. What is it?

148 The German Shepherd dog had its name changed in England and France during and after World War I. What did it become known as?

149 What type of Collie was the Hollywood dog-star, Lassie?

150 What is a "sniffer" dog?

C, C+STANDARD

151 What is a Bobtail better known as?

152 What type of dog was bred to accompany carriages and protect the occupants against highwaymen?

153 What is a Pointer used for?

154 What sort of dog was Rin Tin Tin?

155 What type of terrier is named after the 19th century parson who developed the breed?

B & ABOVE

156 This African hunting dog has

the native name, M'bwa M'kubwa M'bwa Wanwitu or The Jumping-up-and-down Dog. What is it?

157 What is a treeing dog?

158 Sometimes called the Didycoy Dog or the Poacher's Dog, what is this popular sporting dog better known as?

159 Earth dogs is a general term for dogs which hunt burrowing mammals. What is the more familiar term?

160 In what city can be found the monument to Greyfriars Bobby, the Skye Terrier who for 14 years kept vigil on his master's grave?

American/English

America has two distinct styles of riding – Western and English. Most of the eastern half of the country chooses to ride English style, whilst Western riding is preferred for ranching and trail-riding in the West, particularly where long periods in the saddle are required. Whatever the style, there are differences in terminology. This round asks you to give the American equivalent to an English word or phrase.

D, D+ STANDARD
161 Girth.

162 Donkey.

163 Clear round.

164 Off side.

165 Light chestnut.

C, C+ STANDARD
166 Slice of hay.

167 Hunting shirt.

168 Western term for the canter.

169 Good doer.

170 Skewbald.

B & ABOVE
171 Three-day eventing.

172 Headpiece.

173 Hogged mane.

174 Martingale (Western term).

175 Water jump (show jumping).

Colours and Markings

D, D+ STANDARD

176 What colour is a dark bay horse?

177 What is a dappled grey?

178 What is the difference between a piebald and a skewbald?

179 What is a stripe?

180 What is a dorsal stripe?

C, C+ STANDARD

181 What is a snip?

182 How would you recognise an appaloosa?

183 If a black horse has white markings, is it still described as a black horse?

184 What is the difference between a chestnut horse with a blond mane and tail and a palomino?

185 What breed of pony has a mealy muzzle?

B & ABOVE

186 What is another name for a dorsal stripe?

187 What is an Albino?

188 What is the difference between a strawberry roan and a blue roan?

189 What is a wall-eye?

190 Does a dun usually have black points?

Lucky Dip

191 What is an oxer?
    (a) A type of jump
    (b) Another name for a steer
    (c) A cowherd

192 The Pleven, the Tersky and the Shagya are examples of what?
    (a) Riding styles
    (b) Types of Arab horses
    (c) Feeding supplements

193 Where would you find a drawing knife?
    (a) In a farrier's forge – it is used for trimming the foot
    (b) In an artist's studio – it is used for trimming pencils
    (c) In a vet's bag – it is used for lancing an abscess

194 Who rode Aldaniti to victory in the 1981 Grand National?
  (a) Dick Francis
  (b) Terry Biddlecombe
  (c) Bob Champion

195 In what year was the short-format version of the three-day event (ie, without steeplechase or roads and tracks) first introduced at Burghley?
  (a) 2005
  (b) 2006
  (c) 2007

196 How big was Stroller, winner of a silver medal for show jumping at the 1968 Olympic Games and the only pony ever to have won the Hickstead Derby?
  (a) 14hh
  (b) 14.2hh
  (c) 15hh

197 The Pony Express was a group of riders who operated in relay in the early 1860s to carry mail between St Joseph, Missouri, and one other American city. Which one?
  (a) Sacramento
  (b) San Francisco
  (c) Santa Fe

198 Who is credited with developing the "forward seat" in jumping?
  (a) the Duke of Newcastle
  (b) Gervase Markham
  (c) Federico Caprilli

199 In which country is the game of polo supposed to have originated?
  (a) China
  (b) Persia
  (c) Syria

200 Stabled horses need to have succulents added to their daily diet. Which of the following counts as a succulent?
  (a) Carrots
  (b) Rolled oats
  (c) Meadow hay

Quiz No. 3

QUESTIONS ON:

Tack and Turnout; High School Airs
On the Highway; Quotations
Spelling; History of Racing
Lucky Dip

Tack and Turnout

D, D+ STANDARD
201 What is a cavesson?

202 What is the purpose of buckle guards on a saddle?

203 What is a pad saddle?

204 What MUST a hat display if it has been approved by the Pony Club?

205 What is the essential characteristic of a Peacock safety stirrup?

C, C+ STANDARD
206 What is a ported mouthpiece?

207 What is meant by "ratcatcher"?

208 What are "sticky-bum" breeches?

209 What is a bib martingale?

210 What does a Balding girth look like?

B & ABOVE
211 Are spurs with a smooth rotating plastic or rubber ball in the shank permitted in dressage?

212 What should you wear when lungeing a horse?

213 What is the purpose of an Irish Martingale?

214 What is the difference between a Weymouth bit and a Ward Union?

215 What does the BS kite symbol tell you about a riding hat?

High School Airs

D, D+ STANDARD
216 High School is a direct translation of the French name given to this style of horsemanship. What is the French name?

217 Which English king took to High School exercises with great enthusiasm?

218 Describe the *capriole*.

219 What riding school today trains its horses to perform High School airs?

220 Why were these movements considered important in the Middle Ages?

C, C+ STANDARD

221 Describe the *piaffe*.

222 Apart from spurs, which artificial aid was used by High School trainers?

223 Who was the Italian riding master whose training methods made High School airs very popular on the Continent in the 16th century?

224 Why was the mediaeval style of horsemanship ideally suited to using the legs to convey a rider's wishes to his horse?

225 What is meant by the *levade*?

B & ABOVE

226 What is the difference between a *croupade* and a *ballotade*?

227 Who in early 17th century Paris ran a young nobleman's finishing school, with emphasis on equitation?

228 Who was the author of *Gli Ordini di Cavalcare*, published in 1550?

229 What use was made of the pillar or pillars?

230 Why, in the 18th century, was the use of a hedgehog advised as a means of curing a horse of napping?

On The Highway

D, D+ STANDARD

231 When is your pony a "vehicle"?

232 Which side of the road should you use when riding a horse?

233 If you are wearing a stirrup light, which leg should you strap it to and should the front part of the light show red or white?

234 How should you signal when turning right?

235 Are you allowed to ride two abreast on the road?

C, C+ STANDARD

236 How far from the kerb of the road should you ride?

237 When is it safe to change from a walk to a trot and vice versa?

238 On which side of the road should you walk when you have dismounted and are leading your pony?

239 Where should you position your pony when mounting or dismounting on the road?

240 If you have a nervous pony, is it permissible to ride on the grass verge in a residential area?

B & ABOVE

241 If you are leading another horse from your own, should he wear a head collar or a bridle?

242 What signal do you give if you would like another road user (car or lorry) to slow down?

243 The traffic lights ahead are red but, as you get to them, they change to red and amber together. What should you do first?

244 What precaution should you take if riding on the road in frosty weather?

245 How should you proceed round a roundabout?

Quotations: Who said, Who wrote, or Where would you find?

D, D+ STANDARD

246 "A horse, a horse, my Kingdom for a horse."

247 "Tom had a little pony, Jack; He vaulted lightly on its back; And galloped off for miles and miles; A-leaping hedges, gates and stiles."

248 "Ride a cock-horse to Banbury Cross; To see a fair lady upon a white horse."

249 "It ain't the 'unting on the 'ills what 'urts the 'orse's 'ooves but the 'ammer, 'ammer, 'ammer on the 'ard 'igh road."

250 "If you wake at midnight and hear a horse's feet, Don't go drawing back the blind or looking in the street."

C, C+ STANDARD

251 "I had a little pony; his name was Dapple Grey."

252 "For want of a nail the shoe was lost; for want of a shoe the horse was lost; for want of a horse the rider was lost; for want of a rider the kingdom was lost; and all for the want of a horseshoe nail."

253 "No hour of life is lost that is spent in the saddle."

254 "Anyone who is concerned about his dignity would be well advised to keep away from horses."

255 "I freely admit that the best of my fun I owe it to horse and hound."

B & ABOVE

256 "Four things greater than all things are, – Women and Horses and Power and War."

257 "Home is the sailor, home from the sea; And the hunter home from the hill."

258 "It's awf'lly bad luck on Diana; Her ponies have swallowed their bits."

259 "They say princes learn no art truly but the art of horsemanship. The reason is, the brave beast is no flatterer. He will throw a prince as soon as his groom."

260 "A camel is a horse designed by a committee."

Spelling

D, D+ STANDARD

261 Martingale

262 Girth

263 Dartmoor

264 Kimblewick

265 Oxer

C, C+ STANDARD

266 Appaloosa

267 Rhythm

268 Gamgee

269 Surcingle

270 Cavesson

B & ABOVE

272 Oesophagus

273 Akhal-Teke

274 Poultice

275 Azoturia

276 Grakle

History of Racing

D, D+ STANDARD

276 At which racecourse would you find Valentine's Brook?

277 Which important race was won three times by Red Rum?

278 Sir Charles Bunbury and the Earl of Derby tossed a coin in 1776 to decide which of them the new flat race they had just instigated would be named after. Who won?

279 Who was the Darley Arabian?

280 The ghost of which jockey is supposed to haunt Newmarket after he shot himself in 1886?

C, C+ STANDARD

281 At which racecourse would you find The Chair?

282 Which racehorse is known as

21

"The Father of Racing"?

283 What was the name of the first jockey to ride with very short stirrups?

284 Who was the first French racehorse to win the Derby? This happened in 1865.

285 Mandarin won the Grand Steeplechase de Paris at Auteuil in 1962. What was remarkable about his win?

B & ABOVE
286 At which racecourse would you find the Melling Road?

287 In the 1950s which Italian-bred horse twice won the Prix de l'Arc de Triomphe?

288 How old was Lester Piggott when he won his first classic race?

289 Who was the first racehorse owner to transport his horses to a race in a "horsebox" pulled by horses?

290 Which filly won four classic races (all except the Derby in which she was fourth) in 1902?

Lucky Dip

291 What female American film star has ridden across the Gobi Desert in Mongolia?

292 What, in 1949, was described as "the most important horse event in Great Britain"?

293 Who invented side-saddle riding's "leaping-head", the downward curving horn that holds the rider's leg in position?

294 What is a hinny?

295 When travelling a horse in a double trailer, is it better to load him into the right-hand compartment or the left?

296 Historically, what sort of creature was kept in a mews?

297 What is the difference between a bridleway and a byway?

298 What do these numbers have in common: PAS 015, BSEN 1384, ASTM F1163?

299 What percentage of the body of an adult horse is made up of water?

300 Who wrote the poem *The Clipper that stands in the Stall at the Top?*

Quiz No. 4

Abbreviations and Initials

D, D+ STANDARD
What do the following stand for?

301 MFH

302 ODE

303 WWW

304 PPC

305 BSJA

C, C+ STANDARD
306 BE

307 M&M WHP

308 HOYS

309 H&H

310 PDSA

B & ABOVE
311 SHB(GB)

312 AI

313 KWPN

314 DEFRA

315 MFHA

The Stable Yard

D, D+ STANDARD
316 Why should a hay or straw barn be situated, if possible, away from the stable block?

317 What is the minimum size of stable suitable for a pony?

318 If the prevailing wind is from the south-west, should the muck heap be positioned south west or north east of the stable yard?

319 Can you name two areas of the stable yard where good drainage is essential?

320 What can be fitted across the top half of the stable door to discourage a horse from jumping out or to prevent a bad-tempered horse from biting an unwary passer-by?

C, C+ STANDARD
321 What is the recommended minimum width of a stable door?

322 What is an isolation stable?

323 What is the main advantage of using stalls to accommodate several horses?

324 Hay-racks were once a common fitting in a stable. Why is their use now discouraged?

325 Can you suggest a good way of preventing a water bucket from being knocked over?

B & ABOVE
326 What is a "swinging bail"?

327 How high should a stable's doorway be?

328 Who should you go to for advice on the number and positioning of fire extinguishers in a stable yard?

329 What is a "Sheringham" window?

330 How much should a stable floor slope in order to drain properly?

The Seasons

D, D+ STANDARD
331 If your pony lives out, why should you be particularly careful about his diet in the spring?

332 On what date in the autumn does hunting officially begin?

333 Which international three-day event is held at the beginning of May?

334 What should you use to prevent snow from balling in a pony's hooves in winter?

335 Why is a pony more likely to go into a field shelter in the summer than at any other time of the year?

C, C+ STANDARD
336 At what two times of the year does grass show a sudden burst of growth?

337 Ragwort is poisonous to horses. In which months is it particularly prevalent?

338 When does the flat racing season officially end?

339 In which month does the Royal International Horse Show take place?

340 When are the Pony Club Championships?

B & ABOVE
341 When is the Cheltenham Festival?

342 In the northern hemisphere, what is a Thoroughbred racehorse's official birthday?

343 In perfect weather conditions, what determines when the first hay is cut?

344 In winter, what can you put in a horse's drinking trough to discourage the formation of ice?

345 When are hunters "turned away"?

Mouths and Bits

D, D+ STANDARD
346 Does a newborn foal have any teeth at all?

347 How many incisors (front teeth) does a full-grown horse have?

348 What is the space between the incisors and the molars (back teeth) called?

349 What is meant by a jointed snaffle?

350 What is a Pelham bit?

C, C+ STANDARD
351 How many permanent molars (back teeth) does a full-grown horse have?

352 By what name is the blackened depression on the surface or table of the incisor known?

353 What is a tush?

354 What is the snaffle part of a double bridle called?

355 By how much should a well-fitting mouthpiece protrude on either side of the horse's jaw?

B & ABOVE
356 What is Galvayne's groove?

357 At what age does a distinctive hook show on the edge of the upper corner incisor?

358 Why is telling the age of a horse reasonably accurate up to eight years but far more difficult thereafter?

359 What is a hanging-cheek snaffle?

360 On what parts of the horse does a curb bit act?

Horse Breeds

D, D+ STANDARD
361 Which is the smallest of British native ponies?

362 What was a Waler?

363 What horse's outstanding characteristics are its "dish" face, high head and tail carriage, large eyes and lively action?

364 Which European country does

the heavy horse, the Brabant, come from?

365 What breed of horse is exclusively used at the Spanish Riding School in Vienna?

C, C+ STANDARD
366 What is the world's smallest pony?

367 Why is the American Quarter Horse so called?

368 Which Native American tribe developed the Appaloosa?

369 Which British native pony is noted for its "toad" eye?

370 What is the most notable characteristic of the Akhal-Teke horse?

B & ABOVE
371 Where does the Hucul pony come from?

372 How did the American Morgan horse get its name?

373 Why was the gliding gait of the Tennessee Walking Horse developed?

374 At what age is a Connemara pony inspected before being registered in the breed's Stud Book?

375 Which is the only native German pony?

The Derby

D, D+ STANDARD
376 Where is the Derby run?

377 In which century was the Derby founded?

378 What age do Derby runners have to be?

379 Who was the youngest jockey to win the Derby in the 20th century?

380 What is the name of the last bend in the Derby course before the straight run to the finish?

C, C+ STANDARD
381 Sir Charles Bunbury owned the winner of the first Derby. Which horse was that?

382 Are fillies allowed to run in the Derby?

383 What happened to the King's

horse in the Derby of 1913?

384 How long is the Derby?

385 Who was the last horse to win the Derby for the second time?

B & OVER

386 What did many Derby-goers wear in their hats from around 1850 until the fashion died out in the 1880s?

387 In 1844, the Derby was won by Running Rein but the race was subsequently given to Orlando? Why?

388 In the long history of the Derby, nine of the races were run at Newmarket. Why?

389 The best known painting of Derby Day was completed in 1858 and earned for the painter the highest fee at the time ever paid to a living artist. What is his name?

390 What is the name given to the Derby to reflect its importance in the world of racing?

Lucky Dip

391 The Pony Club tetrathlon consists of cross-country riding, swimming, shooting and one other discipline. What is this dicipline?
    (a) cycling
    (b) running
    (c) show jumping

392 Who lives at Badminton where the famous international three-day event is held?
    (a) the Duke of Gloucester
    (b) the Duke of Rutland
    (c) the Duke of Beaufort

393 On a wet day, the cross-country course takes you across a stream via a bridge made of wooden sleepers. How should you cross?
    (a) cross as quickly as you can
    (b) avoid the bridge by jumping the stream
    (c) walk across

394 What is the meaning of the red flag in both cross-country and show jumping?
    (a) You should leave it on your

right
   (b) you should leave it on your left
   (c) you may pass on either side

395 What is is a loriner?
   (a) a lorry-repair specialist
   (b) a maker of bits
   (c) a maker of riding hats

396 When did *Eohippus*, the "Dawn Horse", live on earth?
   (a) 60 million years ago
   (b) 30 million years ago
   (c) 15 thousand years ago

397 What is the meaning of *Equus asinus*?
   (a) an Asian wild horse
   (b) a donkey
   (c) an unbroken colt

398 What is a hackamore?
   (a) a horse used purely for hacking
   (b) a street urchin
   (c) a bitless bridle

399 The word coach comes from the Hungarian *kocsi*, named after the village of Kocs, where a special invention in the 15th century made travel by wagon much less uncomfortable. What was this invention?
   (a) making the front wheels smaller than the back
   (b) making the back wheels smaller than the front
   (c) fitting the wheels with inflatable tyres

400 What was the total weight carried by a mediaeval war-horse, with a rider in full armour?
   (a) 436½lb (224kg)
   (b) 275lb (125kg)
   (c) 122lb (55.45kg)

Quiz No. 5

QUESTIONS ON:

Horses and Royalty; Feet and Shoes
Dogs in General; Farm Animals
Transporting Horses; Horse-drawn Vehicles
Lucky Dip

Horses and Royalty

D, D+ STANDARD

401 What is the name of the Princess Royal's daughter, who is an event rider?

402 The Duke of Edinburgh gave up playing polo when he was 50 years old. What equestrian sport did he take up which led to international success?

403 What was King George VI's favourite equestrian activity?

404 Which King of England died after a fall when his horse tripped over a molehill?

405 Which Queen of England ordered the establishment of a racecourse at Ascot Heath in 1711?

C, C+ STANDARD

406 In whose reign in the 11th century were larger horses brought from the Continent to supplement the native Celtic ponies?

407 On what horse did Princess Anne win the European eventing championship in 1971?

408 Which recent member of the Royal Family was a keen supporter of steeplechasing and owned many successful steeplechase horses?

409 What were racehorses called in the early Middle Ages?

410 In the 18th century, what happened to the deer released for the King to hunt?

B & ABOVE

411 Whose nickname was Old Rowley, after whom the Rowley Mile at Newmarket racecourse was named?

412 Who was the first English king to appoint a Royal Horsemaster?

413 Queen Alexandra was left after a bout of rheumatic fever with a stiff right knee which made it impossible for her to ride side-saddle in the orthodox way. What did she do to ensure that she could carry on riding side-saddle?

414 Queen Elizabeth I, although she enjoyed riding, never rode a spirited "courser", popular with the nobles at court. Instead, her mount was "a small animal of gentle disposition". What type of horse was this?

415 Which Queen of England had a favourite pony, a "little, dark-brown horse with a springy action" called Tartar?

Feet and Shoes

D, D+ STANDARD

416 What is the rubbery, V-shaped part of the underside of the hoof called?

417 How many toes on each foot did the ancestor of today's horses, Meohippus, who lived about 25 million years ago, have?

418 What is meant if a horse is described as pigeon-toed?

419 What is a clench?

420 When using a hoofpick, should you work it towards you or away from you?

C, C+ STANDARD

421 Where is the coronary band?

422 The first single-toed horse was Pliohippus, which lived how many million years ago?

423 What is the wall of the foot?

424 What is a T-tap?

425 Are shoes essential for all horses in general use?

B & ABOVE

426 The "Dawn Horse", Eohippus, who was around about 60 million years ago, had toes instead of a hoof. How many on the front feet and how many on the hind?

427 What shape of foot can lead to corns, tendon strain, bruising and navicular?

428 Which stud, pointed or square, would you choose for jumping in hard, dry conditions?

429 What is the difference between a grasscrack and a sandcrack?

430 Who used sandals made of grass on their horses?

Dogs in General

D, D+ STANDARD

431 What was the name of the dog in Enid Blyton's *Famous Five* series?

432 What is a foxhound's tail called?

433 A dog cannot sweat. What does he do instead?

434 What is the name of the dog owned by Charlie Brown?

435 He spent 30 years as a dogfood salesman before founding the Dog Show which bears his name. Who was he?

C, C+ STANDARD

436 What did a dog called Pickles find under a bush in South London in 1966?

437 Which animal charity was originally known as Our Dumb Friends' League?

438 For showing purposes, how old does a dog have to be before it can compete in Veteran Classes?

439 What is a the gestation period of a bitch?

440 Are a dog's senses of smell and hearing better developed than its eyesight?

B & ABOVE

441 During the War of Independence, General Washington called a special truce to return something of value to the British commander, General Howe. What was it?

442 What is a dog's normal temperature?

443 What does the Latin term, *cave canem*, mean?

444 What is the name of the dog in the cartoon series, *Asterix*?

445 Who was Toto?

Farm Animals

D, D+ STANDARD

446 What type of animal is a Southdown?
    (a) a sheep
    (b) a pig
    (c) a cow

447 Where did turkeys come from originally?
    (a) North Africa
    (b) Turkey
    (c) North America

448 What colour is a Rhode Island Red chicken?
    (a) brown
    (b) black
    (c) speckled

449 Foot-and-Mouth disease affects what type of animal?
    (a) horses
    (b) ducks and geese
    (c) all cloven-hoofed animals

450 If cows are polled, what does this mean?

    (a) they have no horns

    (b) they have very prominent foreheads

    (c) they are allowed to choose their own milking stall

C, C+ STANDARD

451 What type of animal is a Middle White?

    (a) a sheep

    (b) a pig

    (c) a cow

452 What type of domestic livestock first appeared in China around 1400BC?

    (a) cattle

    (b) poultry

    (c) goats

453 What colour are Aberdeen Angus cattle?

    (a) white

    (b) black and white

    (c) black

454 What is meant by the term "feral"?

    (a) undersized animals

    (b) livestock kept indoors

    (c) domestic livestock which has returned to the wild

455 What is the average weight of a fully grown Large Black boar?

    (a) 500kg

    (b) 350kg

    (c) 750kg

B & ABOVE

456 What type of animal is a Saanen?

    (a) a pig

    (b) a cow

    (c) a goat

457 What is the smallest breed of cattle?

    (a) Dexter

    (b) Hereford

    (c) Charollais

458 Which animals are attacked by the disease known as Anaplasmosis, which is carried by ticks?

    (a) goats

    (b) poultry

    (c) cattle

459 What is the standard length of a hank of wool?

    (a) 512m (500 yds)

    (b) 360m (300 yds)

    (c) 76m (83 yds)

460 The Muscovy is descended from the wild Musk Duck which lived in

    (a) Southern Europe

    (b) South America

    (c) China?

Transporting Horses

D, D+ STANDARD

461 For nearly 100 years, until the 1920s, what, other than hacking, was the most popular method of taking a horse to a distant destination?

462 What is a breast bar?

463 Is it legal for a person to travel in a moving trailer?

464 What should be inspected first when buying a second-hand trailer?

465 Why do you put a tail bandage on a horse when travelling?

C, C+ STANDARD

466 If your horse has to travel long distances or abroad, what three methods of travel are available to you?

467 What is a breeching strap?

468 What is the maximum speed at which a trailer may be towed?

469 Which part of a trailer floor is most susceptible to rot?

470 What is the purpose of a poll-guard?

B & ABOVE

471 With winds of Force 7 and above can a sea captain refuse to carry horses on his ship?

472 What is the jockey wheel?

473 How do you find out a vehicle's maximum legal towing weight?

474 What is the average height from the ground of the towball on a towing vehicle?

475 Should elastic bandages be used to protect the legs when travelling?

Horse-drawn Vehicles

D, D+ STANDARD

476 What is a four-in-hand?

477 Can you name an animal, other than a horse or pony, which might be used to draw a light cart?

478 What is a buggy?

479 Name an item of transport, past or present, which can use horses to pull it but is not used on the road.

480 What type of horse drew a hackney carriage?

C, C+ STANDARD

481 What is a troika?

482 A budget, a boot and an imperial were all names for what?

483 What was a prairie schooner?

484 What kind of company most commonly used a dray for making deliveries?

485 What is meant by using horses "in tandem"?

B & ABOVE

486 When would you use a pole rather than shafts to draw a vehicle?

487 What is a diligence?

488 Describe a travois.

489 What was a phaeton?

490 Why were hansom cabs so called?

Lucky Dip

491 What is a groundline?

492 What does the use of electrolytes regulate?

493 What is the name of the military troop which fires ceremonial salutes on State Occasions?

494 Who is responsible for checking that every horse-owner has his horse's passport?

495 What was a destrier?

496 Who wrote "A horse is dangerous at both ends and uncomfortable in the middle"?

497 Why should a horse's travelling rug be secured with a roller?

498 What is a "good doer"?

499 What is the sequence of footfalls at the walk?

500 How long is a standard whip?

Answers

QUIZ No. 1

Horse and Pony Care

1 At least once a day.

2 Soak it in cold water (three parts water to one part pulp) for 12 hours and, once prepared, feed it within 24 hours.

3 It is used for cleaning the body brush.

4 No, but both grass and hay should be of good quality.

5 Grooming should be limited to when the pony is being ridden. Even then, it should be sufficient to remove mud and sweat marks, and tangles from mane and tail. The feet should be picked out and shoes inspected, and sponges used on eyes, nose, muzzle and dock.

6 A routine whereby a stabled pony is turned out to grass every day.

7 At least 1½ hours.

8 It is designed to remove dust and scurf from the body, mane and tail.

9 From about 15% of his daily intake for a 12hh pony to 33.3% for a 16hh horse, divided into two or three feeds per day.

10 To remove dried mud or sweat.

11 Potassium.

12 Pallets allow air to circulate beneath the hay and straw and prevent damp from penetrating the bales.

13 Approximately 15kg or 33lbs.

14 Oat straw, which is nutritionally better than very poor hay.

15 To massage the horse. The wisp helps him to develop and harden the muscles. It stimulates the supply of blood to the skin and makes the coat shine.

The Numbers Game

16 1½ miles.

17 Three.

18 Ten thousand.

19 Four.

20 Eight years old upwards.

21 1780.

22 37.5ºC (99.5ºF) to 38.5ºC (101.3ºF).

23 600.

24 Four.

25 3-3.6m (10-12ft)

26 1776.

27 200 beats.

28 About 300,000.

29 45-50º.

30 3.6m (12ft) square.

The Countryside

31 Headland.

32 No. You should always leave a gate as you found it.

33 Late spring – ie, April-May.

34 Guidelines as to how to treat the countryside. For members of the public, these are:
– Be safe, plan ahead and follow any signs.
– Leave gates and property as you find them
– Protect plants and animals and take your litter home
– Keep dogs under close control
– Consider other people.

35 Pull it up by the roots, preferably before it flowers, and BURN it. It is poisonous to horses.

36 Your horse may trip on exposed roots and you may get hit in the face or swept out of the saddle by a low-hanging branch.

37 An Equinox is when day and night are the same length. A Solstice is when the hours of daylight are at their longest (summer) or shortest (winter).

38 A cart has two wheels; a wagon has four.

39 Meadow Fescue, Timothy, Rye Grass, Crested Dog's-tail, Cocksfoot.

40 At least 1½ acres. If the grazing is good and the pasture properly cared for, one acre per pony would be sufficient.

41 Get down and roll. Kick him on!

42 An ancient track used in the past by herdsmen moving sheep or cattle from one area to another.

43 Fallow deer, Red deer, Roe deer, Muntjac, Sika deer.

44 Every month, as in a heavily gorse-ridden area there will always be some gorse in bloom. Common gorse flowers profusely between February and May.

45 The horse-fly. (This is the Latin name.)

Around the World

46 America. It is a feral horse of the prairies.

47 On the pampas, or plains, of South America. They are cowboys.

48 Camargue horses, who are mostly grey.

49 Kentucky.

50 Cossacks.

51 The Royal International Horse Show.

52 Looks after the ponies. He is a groom.

53 Brazil, South America.

54 Vienna, Austria.

55 Mustangs.

56 Mongolia.

57 The Maryland Hunt Cup, whose post-and-rail fences are built of solid timber.

58 In Australia. It is the name given to the feral horses of that continent.

59 A troika.

60 The Argentine.

Ancient Times

61 Pegasus.

62 The Book of Job (Ch.39, vv 19-25).

63 About as big as a small fox.

64 Diana.

65 Bucephalus.

66 Asiatic wild ass.

67 The Scythians.

68 The Celts.

69 The Romans.

70 Artemis

71 Ullr.

72 Xenophon.

73 The Arab.

74 Around 4,000BC.

75 Pliohippus, which lived about 10 million years ago.

Health and Safety

76 (b) Crouch down.

77 (a) When competing across country in a Pony club event.

78 (c) Both.

79 (c) Cut it into finger-shaped pieces.

80 (a) Run your hand down the back of the leg and lean against it.

81 (b) Tie the haynet to a string loop, using a quick-release knot.

82 All three.

83 (b) Wait before offering him water.

84 (a) A Peacock safety stirrup.

85 (b) Walk along the left-hand side of the road, leading on the offside of the pony.

86 (c) 17 or above.

87 (b) 1965.

88 (c) A qualified first-aider.

89 (a) A body protector and a medical armband.

90 (c) Leave the hat on and place rider in recovery position.

Lucky Dip

91 Mr Douglas Bunn.

92 Epsom Racecourse.

93 Celtic goddess, patroness of horse-breeders.

94 A group of 14 races for Thoroughbreds, held annually at a different location in the United States on different surfaces and over different distances.

95 The Breton.

96 In Les Invalides in Paris.

97 *Black Beauty*, by Anna Sewell.

98 Season of the year (usually the breeding season) when the hunting or shooting of game is forbidden

99 Cavalry.

100 To tear at grass.

QUIZ No. 2

The Pony Club

101 The E Test.

102 Anyone aged 21 years or under who rides at a riding school as a recognised Pony Club Centre and who does not own a pony.

103 White.

104 Feed your Pony, Points of the Pony, Points of Tack, Birds, Grooming, Road Sense, Horse Clothing, Farming, Poisonous Plants, Pony Behaviour, Care of the Foot, Working Dogs.

105 1929.

106 Small booklets designed to help members pass their Achievement Badges.

107 19.

108 Nothing. The Pony Club's policy is not to award money prizes in competitions open only to Pony Club members.

109 North West Kent, in 1957.

110 Yes.

111 The Tailwaggers' Club in the *Daily Express*.

112 The Examiner and the District Commissioner of the Branch conducting the Test.

113 1997.

114 The Royal Calpe Hunt Branch, Gibraltar, in 1930.

115 Connecticut.

Horses in Fiction

116 The Pie.

117 Silver.

118 Champion.

119 Black Beauty.

120 Jack.

121 The Maltese Cat.

122 Rosinante.

123 Merrylegs.

124 Boxer.

125 Right Royal.

126 Lollo.

127 Modestine.

128 The Red Pony.

129 Houyhnhnms.

130 Flicka.

At the Races

131 Aintree.

132 Five furlongs.

133 Five – the 2,000 Guineas, the 1,000 Guineas, the Derby, the Oaks and the St. Leger.

134 The British Horseracing Authority (BHA).

135 It has a tassel on the top.

136 An apprentice or conditional jockey who has not yet won enough races to carry the full weight and can claim a reduction according to the number of races he has won.

137 Newmarket.

138 Doncaster.

139 Betting system, similar to the Tote, which operates in French racing.

140 40.

141 The Kentucky Derby, the Belmont Stakes and the Preakness Stakes.

142 Longchamp, Paris.

143 Ascot.

144 20 races.

145 A flat race for jump jockeys at a National Hunt meeting.

Working Dogs

146 A hare.

147 Welsh Corgi (Pembroke).

148 Alsatian.

149 Rough Collie.

150 A dog trained to detect illegal drugs.

151 Old English Sheepdog.

152 Dalmatian.

153 To indicate where hares or other game might be hiding.

154 German Shepherd Dog.

155 Jack Russell.

156 Basenji.

157 Developed in America, this is a dog trained to bark at the bottom of the tree in which its prey – usually raccoon or opossum – has taken shelter and to wait there until the hunters have caught up with it.

158 Lurcher.

159 Terrier.

160 Edinburgh.

American/English

161 Cinch.

162 Ass.

163 Clean round.

164 Far side.

165 Sorrel.

166 Flake of hay.

167 Ratcatcher.

168 Lope.

169 Easy keeper.

170 Pinto or paint.

171 Combined training.

172 Headstall.

173 Roach.

174 Tie-down.

175 Liverpool (that is, an obstacle containing a water element).

Colours and Markings

176 Dark brown with black points (black legs, mane and tail).

177 A grey horse or pony where the grey colouring forms circular patterns in the coat.

178 A piebald is white with black patches; a skewbald is white with patches of any other colour except black.

179 A narrow white mark running down the horse's face.

180 A dark line along a pony's back from withers to tail.

181 A white mark between the nostrils.

182 A spotted horse, either white with coloured spots or coloured with white spots.

183 Yes.

184 A palomino's mane and tail are

white. If the mane and tail are a pale golden colour, even though they are lighter than the body colour, the horse would be described as a chestnut.

185 Exmoor pony.

186 Eel stripe, back stripe, lineback, list.

187 A true Albino has a white coat, pink skin and pink eyes but there are no true Albino horses or ponies. There is a white horse, bred in America, but it has blue or brown eyes and is therefore not a true Albino.

188 A roan is a horse or pony whose basic coloured coat has white hairs mixed in with it. Thus a strawberry roan is chestnut mixed with white and a blue roan is black mixed with white.

189 A pale blue eye instead of the normal brown one.

190 Yes.

Lucky Dip

191 (a) A type of jump.

192 (b) Types of Arab horse.

193 (a) It is used for trimming the foot.

194 (c) Bob Champion.

195 (c) 2006.

196 (b) 14.2hh.

197 (a) Sacramento.

198 (c) Federico Caprilli.

199 (b) Persia.

200 (a) Carrots.

QUIZ No. 3

Tack and Turnout

201 A type of noseband.

202 To prevent damage to the saddle from the girth buckles.

203 A saddle made of thick felt without a tree, mainly used for small ponies.

204 A purple tag wrapped round part of the chinstrap.

205 One side consists of a removable, thick rubber ring.

206 An inverted U-shaped curve in the centre of a bit's mouthpiece. It acts on the roof of the mouth and, in the wrong hands, makes the bit quite severe.

207 Informal dress (ie. tweed jacket instead of black or red) worn when autumn hunting.

208 Breeches which have an insert in the seat and thighs made of suede leather or similar fabric. It is meant to prevent slipping about in the saddle.

209 A type of running martingale in which a V-shaped piece of leather is inserted where the two straps of the martingale divide.

210 Made of leather, it has a centre portion split into three, with the outside straps crossed over and stitched. It is designed is to make the girth narrower behind the elbow.

211 Yes.

212 You should be tidily dressed at all times and formally dressed if doing a test. An approved hat and gloves are essential. Spurs should not be worn.

213 Strictly speaking, not a martingale at all, it is a short strip of leather with a ring at each end through which the reins pass. It helps to ensure that the pull on the reins is in the right direction and prevents the reins from coming over the horse's head should horse or rider fall.

214 A Weymouth bit has a sliding mouthpiece.

215 It tells you that the hat has been batch tested for impact and that the hat meets the standards laid down.

High School Airs

216 Haute école.

217 Henry VIII.

218 A movement in which the horse leaps into the air and lashes out with his hind-legs.

219 The Spanish Riding School, Vienna.

220 They were believed to benefit the cavalry when at war.

221 A collected trot on the spot.

222 Pillars to which a horse in training could be attached, either to one pillar or between two.

223 Federico Grisone.

224 Mediaeval knights carried so much in their hands (shield, lance etc) that the use of the reins to guide the horse was limited. Riders relied on their legs to control their mounts, leg-aids being often supplemented by cruel spurs.

225 This is the movement in which the horse raises his forehand off the ground and lowers his hindlegs so that he forms an angle of 30-35° to the ground. It requires great strength and precision from the horse.

226 In a *croupade*, the horse leaps into the air, drawing his hindlegs up towards his belly; the *ballotade* is similar except that the horse turns his hind feet up so that the shoes are visible.

227 Antoine de Pluvinel.

228 Federico Grisone.

229 The horse was tied to a single pillar and taught high school airs as he moved round it. Similarly, he could be tethered between two pillars to teach movements like the *ballotade* or the *capriole*.

230 A hedgehog would be tied under the horse's tail causing him to rush forward to try to get away from it. Unfortunately, this method often brought about a worse vice than napping – bolting!

On The Highway

231 When he is being ridden or led along a road.

232 The left hand or near side, the same as a bicycle or car.

233 It should be strapped to your right leg. It should show white to the front, red to the rear.

234 Extend your right arm out at right angles, level with your shoulder.

235 Yes, on a wide, straight, quiet

road, but you should always watch out for cars behind you and move into single file to let them pass.

236 About one pony's width from the kerb.

237 When you can see and be seen and you feel it is safe to do so.

238 You should still walk on the left or near side but position yourself between your pony and the traffic.

239 Find a place where there is plenty of room, such as a gateway, bus stop or wide verge, in case your pony swings round.

240 No.

241 His bridle as this gives you more control.

242 Put your arm out straight, with the palm of hand facing downwards and raise and lower it several times.

243 Stop. You should move off only when the light turns to green.

244 Put knee boots on the pony and road studs in his shoes. If you come across a wide patch of ice, dismount and lead your pony across.

245 Wait at the "give-way" line until

the road to the right is clear. Then walk round the roundabout, keeping to left-hand side. Signal right when approaching an exit you do not want to take and left when you do want to leave the roundabout. Check behind you on both sides before turning left.

Quotations – Who said, Who wrote, or Where would you find?

246 Richard III.

247 Hilaire Belloc (*New Cautionary Tales for Children*).

248 It is a nursery rhyme.

249 Jorrocks in a book by R S Surtees.

250 Rudyard Kipling (from *Smugglers' Song* in *Puck of Pook's Hill*).

251 It is a nursery rhyme.

252 Benjamin Franklin (from *Poor Richard's Almanac*).

253 Winston Churchill.

254 HRH Prince Philip, Duke of Edinburgh.

255 George Whyte-Melville (from *The Good Grey Mare*).

256 Rudyard Kipling (from *Ballad of*

the King's Jest).

257 R L Stevenson (from *Requiem*).

258 John Betjeman.

259 Ben Jonson.

260 Proverb, quoted by Sir Alec Issigonis.

Spelling

261 MARTINGALE.

262 GIRTH.

263 DARTMOOR.

264 KIMBLEWICK.

265 OXER.

266 APPALOOSA.

267 RHYTHM.

268 GAMGEE.

269 SURCINGLE.

270 CAVESSON.

271 OESOPHAGUS.

272 AKHAL-TEKE.

273 POULTICE.

274 AZOTURIA.

275 GRAKLE.

History of Racing

276 Aintree.

277 Grand National.

278 The Earl of Derby.

279 One of the three 17th century stallions imported from the Middle East from whom all Thoroughbred racehorses are descended.

280 Fred Archer.

281 Aintree.

282 Eclipse, foaled in 1764 during an eclipse of the sun, who was never beaten and who sired 335 winners.

283 Tod Sloan, American jockey born in 1874, who was nicknamed "The Monkey on a Stick".

284 Gladiateur, in 1865. A statue of him stands in the paddock at Longchamp, Paris.

285 His bit broke after the third fence. His jockey, Fred Winter, rode him the remaining three miles to victory without a bridle!

286 Aintree.

287 Ribot. He was unbeaten in all seventeen of his races as a two-, three-and four-year-old.He became a successful sire of Classic winners.

288 18 years old (he won the Epsom Derby on Never Say Die in 1954).

289 Lord George Bentinck (1802-1848) who in 1836 devised a horse-drawn wagon in which he conveyed his St Leger runner, Elis, 224 miles from Goodwood to Doncaster, thus keeping the horse fresh for the race, which Elis won.

290 Signorinetta.

Lucky Dip

291 Julia Roberts, star of such films as *Pretty Woman*.

292 Badminton Horse Trials.

293 Thomas Oldaker, a professional huntsman, who at the end of the 18th century was compelled by injury to ride side-saddle and invented the "leaping head" to help keep him in place.

294 The offspring of a donkey mother and a horse father.

295 The right-hand side of the trailer: it will give the horse a better ride.

296 Birds of prey used in falconry.

297 A bridleway is a countryside track or path over which the public have the right to travel on foot or on horseback, but on which no vehicles of any kind are allowed. A byway can be of two types: an unsurfaced countryside track that is open to all traffic (BOAT) or a restricted byway open to users of wheeled traffic (horse-drawn vehicles or bicycles) but not open to any mechanically-propelled vehicle.

298 They are all numbers applied to and printed inside riding hats to show that they conform to certain standards.

299 Approximately 65%.

300 G J Whyte-Melville.

QUIZ No. 4

Abbreviations and Initials

301 Master of Foxhounds.

302 One-Day Event.

303 world wide web.

304 Prince Philip Cup.

305 British Show Jumping Association.

306 British Eventing.

307 Mountain and Moorland Working Hunter Pony.

308 Horse of the Year Show.

309 *Horse & Hound.*

310 People's Dispensary for Sick Animals.

311 Sport Horse Breeding of Great Britain.

312 Assistant Instructor (BHS teaching qualification).

313 Initials by which the Royal Warmblood Studbook of the Netherlands is known.

314 Department for Environment, Food and Rural Affairs.

315 Master of Foxhounds Association.

The Stable Yard

316 To minimise the risk of a fire in the hay barn from spreading to the stables and to keep the stables as dust-free as possible.

317 3.6m (12ft) by 3m (10ft).

318 North east.

319 In loose boxes and stalls, beneath taps and in any area where horses or vehicles may be hosed down.

320 A grille.

321 1.1m (about 3ft 7ins).

322 A stable separated from the rest where a horse with a contagious illness can be isolated.

323 More horses or ponies can be kept in the space available.

324 It was found that by forcing horses to look up when a rack was fixed above head level, dust and hay seeds fell into their eyes. A hay rack at chest level is not a problem.

325 Bucket holders are available from

saddlers and feed stores. A less expensive alternative is to place the bucket in an old car tyre of a suitable size.

326 This is a plank or pole the length of the stall, suspended at both ends from the ceiling so that it forms a barrier between two horses. It must be high enough to prevent a horse from getting his leg over it, slightly higher at the back than the front and secured by a quick-release knot to ensure a rapid removal in an emergency.

327 Not less than 2.1m (7ft).

328 A local fire officer, who will give advice.

329 A window in which the top half is hinged along the bottom of its frame so that it can open inwards. This directs fresh air upwards and prevents draughts.

330 The slope on a stable floor should not be greater than is necessary for liquids to drain away properly. A slope of 1 in 48 is best.

The Seasons

331 Ponies are notoriously greedy and will overeat when the new spring grass comes in. This can cause inflammation of the laminae and the onset of laminitis, a potentially fatal and exceedingly painful disease of the foot. Try to keep your pony on a "starvation paddock" where the grazing is poor and allow him access to the good grass for very short periods.

332 November 1st.

333 Badminton.

334 Butter spread on the sole of the foot is excellent for preventing snow from balling. But if your mother objects, axle grease (from the local garage) is also effective.

335 To get away from flies. He is more likely in winter to stand outside the shelter where he is protected from the wind.

336 March/April and September, commonly known as the Spring Flush and the Autumn Flush.

337 June and July. It should be pulled up by the roots and burned.

338 November officially, although nowadays with all-weather tracks some flat racing continues throughout the winter.

339 July.

340 End of August.

341 March.

342 January 1st.

343 Hay should be cut in dry sunny weather when the grass is coming into flower and before it has gone to seed.

344 A rubber ball, which bounces about in the water and inhibits the formation of ice.

345 During the summer months, the close season. They are usually turned out with shoes removed, although some may be shod in front to prevent the hooves from cracking. Even though they may not be ridden, "turned-away" hunters should still be checked every day.

Mouths and Bits

346 Yes, but they are often covered by a thin membrane.

347 12.

348 Bars of the mouth.

349 A snaffle bit in which the mouthpiece is in two halves, joined by a central link.

350 The Pelham is an attempt to combine the actions of both parts of the double bridle in a single bit. It is best used with two reins, the upper one attached to the snaffle ring of the bit, the lower one, the curb rein, attached to the ring at the bottom of the curb shank. Pressure on the upper rein causes the bit to act on the bars of the mouth, the corners and the tongue. Pressure on the curb rein transfers pressure to the poll. The longer the shank the greater the pressure.

351 24.

352 Mark.

353 A single canine tooth which appears around the age of four or five between the incisors and the molars. There are usually two in the bottom jaw and two in the top and as a rule only appear in male horses or ponies.

354 A bridoon.

355 About 5mm (¼in).

356 A furrow which appears at the top of the outer incisor when a horse is about ten years old and reaches the biting edge of the tooth when he reaches 20 or 25. After that it gradually disappears.

357 At seven years old. It is sometimes called the "seven-year hook".

358 Changes in the teeth are much more gradual after a horse has reached the age of eight and it is therefore more difficult to pinpoint the age he has become.

359 A snaffle bit which is suspended in the mouth rather than resting on the tongue.

360 The curb bit acts principally on the poll but also on the bars of the mouth, the tongue and the chin groove.

Horse Breeds

361 Shetland.

362 An Australian horse, from New South Wales. It was the forerunner of the Australian Stock Horse.

363 Arab.

364 Belgium.

365 Lipizzaner.

366 Falabella.

367 The Quarter Horse, bred by crossing Spanish horses with English Thoroughbreds, was renowned for his ability to show dazzling speed over a quarter of a mile. It led to his being used all over America for this type of sprint racing. He was also capable of stopping and turning at will and this made him an excellent cow horse. As longer races grew in popularity, sprint racing was abandoned and only held from time to time in the Western States, while the Quarter Horse continued to be the pony of choice by cowboys. Today Quarter Horse racing is growing popular again.

368 The Nez Percé tribe.

369 The Exmoor.

370 The golden sheen of its coat.

371 Poland.

372 All Morgan horses are descended from a colt given to an innkeeper named Justin Morgan in the 1790s in settlement of a debt. He was only about 14hh but a strong and willing worker and although his real name was Figure he was always known as Justin Morgan's horse. His most useful ability, however, was that his offspring all took after him, being compact, strong and willing, so that today the Morgan still resembles his ancestor and is a handsome, all-purpose family horse.

373 The Tennessee Walking Horse has a fluid gliding gait which makes him particularly comfortable to ride.

This gait was developed by selective breeding to provide plantation owners with a horse on which they could sit happily all day when touring their plantations, and one which was stylish in appearance and possessed of great stamina.

374 Two years old.

375 The Dulmen pony.

The Derby

376 Epsom.

377 18th century.

378 Three years old.

379 Lester Piggott.

380 Tattenham Corner.

381 Diomed.

382 Yes.

383 He was brought down by a suffragette, who threw herself under the horses just before Tattenham Corner. She was killed. The horse was all right.

384 1½ miles.

385 A trick question. The Derby cannot be won twice because it is open only to three-year-olds.

386 A little wooden doll with movable arms and legs, which was tucked into the hatband. It would be bought from a pedlar on the racecourse for one old penny and worn during the races and all next day. Some racegoers bought several and wore them all round their hats.

387 Running Rein turned out to be a four-year-old named Maccabaeus and therefore ineligible for the Derby. Orlando had finished second.

388 They were the Derbies (1915-1918 and 1940-1945) run during the two World Wars.

389 William Powell Frith was commissioned to paint *Derby Day* for £1,500 guineas. His patron was Jacob Bell, a wealthy pharmacist and an old friend of Frith's. Frith subsequently sold engraving rights for a further £1,500 and sole exhibition rights for £750. Five thousand and twenty-five copies of the engraving were on sale to the public for prices ranging from five to fifteen guineas.

390 It was described in 1848 by Benjamin Disraeli as "The Blue

Riband of the Turf".

Lucky Dip

391 (b) Running.

392 (c) The Duke of Beaufort.

393 (c) Walk across. The bridge is likely to be very slippery.

394 (a) You should leave it on your right.

395 (b) A maker of bits.

396 (a) 60 million years ago.

397 (b) A domestic donkey.

398 (c) A bitless bridle.

399 (a) Making the front wheels smaller than the back.

400 (a) 436½lb (224kg).

QUIZ No. 5

Horses and Royalty

401 Zara Phillips.

402 Driving, particularly four-in-hands.

403 Hunting.

404 William III.

405 Queen Anne.

406 William the Conqueror, William I.

407 Doublet.

408 Queen Elizabeth the Queen Mother.

409 Running horses.

410 Hounds would be called off, the deer caught, fed and bedded down for the night before being returned to the deer paddocks. Many of the stags were given names and released for "hunting" several times a season and for several seasons.

411 Charles II.

412 Alfred the Great.

413 She moved the pommel to the offside of the saddle and sat with her legs to the right.

414 A palfrey.

415 Queen Victoria.

Feet and Shoes

416 The frog.

417 Three.

418 He has feet which turn in.

419 A horseshoe nail.

420 Away from you.

421 At the top of the hoof. It is the part from which the horn grows.

422 Ten million.

423 The thick horn that encloses the foot.

424 The tool used for fitting studs into shoes.

425 No, provided the feet are tough and well-shaped and the horse has little roadwork to do.

426 Four on the front and three on the hind.

427 Flat, sloping feet.

428 Pointed studs are best when the ground is hard and dry.

429 The grasscrack is a split growing upwards from bottom of the foot, not uncommon if the hooves are overlong. The sandcrack is also a split but it grows downwards from the coronary band and is harder to treat.

430 The Ancient Greeks.

Dogs in General

431 Timmy.

432 Stern.

433 He loses heat by panting and letting his tongue hang out of his mouth.

434 Snoopy.

435 Charles Cruft.

436 Football's World Cup which had been stolen a few weeks earlier.

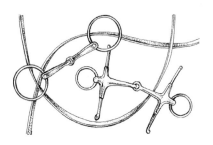

437 The Blue Cross.

438 Seven years old.

439 About 8-9 weeks.

440 Yes.

441 A foxhound belonging to the English general. He had strayed into the American lines and was identified by an inscription on his collar.

442 38.5°C (101.5°F).

443 Beware of the dog.

444 Dogmatrix.

445 Dorothy's dog in *The Wizard of Oz*.

Farm Animals

446 (a) A sheep.

447 (c) North America.

448 (a) Brown.

449 (c) All cloven-footed animals.

450 (a) They have no horns.

451 (b) A pig.

452 (b) Poultry.

453 (c)Black.

454 (c) Domestic livestock which has returned to the wild.

455 (a) 500kg.

456 (c) Goat.

457 (a) Dexter.

458 (c) Cattle.

459 (a) 512m (560 yds).

460 (b) South America.

Transporting Horses

461 Horses were transported by train.

462 It is a removable bar, which fits across the trailer at chest height to prevent the horse or horses from moving forwards, particularly if the trailer stops suddenly.

463 No.

464 The floor.

465 To prevent the top of the tail from getting rubbed.

466 Rail, sea or air, the latter being the most popular method these days of taking horses abroad.

467 A strap which is fastened behind a horse to prevent him from backing out once loaded or when the ramp is lowered.

468 60 mph (96kph) but 40mph (68kph) to 50mph (80kph) is safer.

469 Corners of trailers are particularly susceptible because straw tends to build up there and the wood does not dry out properly.

470 To protect the horse's head if he throws it up and hits the trailer while being loaded or unloaded.

471 Yes.

472 This the single wheel at the front of a trailer which can be raised or lowered to hitch or unhitch a trailer. It is lowered to the ground to balance the trailer when stationary and raised out of harm's way when the trailer is ready to move off.

473 The information should be contained in the towing vehicle's documents. If they are not available, a car dealer or garage should be able to tell you.

474 18in (46cm).

475 No. If bandages are used instead of travelling boots, they should be applied with padding under the bandage and continued down the leg to cover and protect the coronary band.

Horse-drawn Vehicles

476 Carriage drawn by four horses.

477 Donkey, goat or dog.

478 It is a lightweight carriage with two or four wheels, drawn by one or two horses. It usually has a folding top. The term is used more in America than in the UK.

479 Canal boats, coal wagons pulled by pit ponies, agricultural vehicles such as ploughs or seed drills, army vehicles – eg, gun carriage, etc.

480 High stepping horse or pony. Nowadays seen at shows with a Hackney horse or pony between the shafts.

481 Russian sledge drawn by three horses.

482 They are all leather travelling cases.

483 Covered wagon used by American pioneers as they opened up the western areas of America.

484 Breweries.

485 Horses harnessed one behind the other are said to be in tandem.

486 When the vehicle is pulled by a pair or several pairs of horses working side by side. The pole passes between the pairs.

487 This is a term used for a type of French stage coach.

488 A V-shaped wheel-less frame which was drawn by men, dogs or horses with the open ends of the V dragging on the ground. It is more manoeuvrable on rough terrain that a cart with wheels. It was used by the Native American tribes, notably the Plains Indians.

489 A sporty, four-wheeled carriage with large wheels which was both fast and dangerous. It was very popular with young men in Regency times.

490 They were called after their designer, Joseph Hansom, a Leicestershire architect, who wanted a fast, safe carriage that could be

pulled by one horse. The driver sat on a sprung seat at the rear. They were valuable as vehicles for hire, the equivalent of today's taxis.

Lucky Dip

491 The groundline is the base of a fence and enables the horse to judge his take-off point, A pole on the ground, pulled forward slightly, will prevent the horse from getting too close to the jump. The groundline does not have to be a pole or right on the ground. The base of a solid filler, such as a wall or the lowest pole of a triple bar, will do instead.

492 The horse's body fluids.

493 The King's Troop the Royal Horse Artillery.

494 The local Trading Standards Office.

495 A mediaeval warhorse. About 14.2-15.2hh, he was strong and muscular and capable of carrying a knight in full armour.

496 This well-known comment is attributed to Ian Fleming, author of the James Bond books.

497 This is to prevent the rug from slipping round while travelling which could cause the horse to panic.

498 A horse or pony which keeps weight on and feeds well and whose condition is easy to maintain.

499 The sequence is:
(1) left hind,
(2) left fore,
(3) right hind
(4) right fore.

500 74cm (2ft 6in).